Head, shoulders, knees & toes

Lobo loved to play all day. He forgot to take care of his body when he went out to play.

He played from morning to evening and always came home with cuts and bruises. Lobo's parents were always worried.

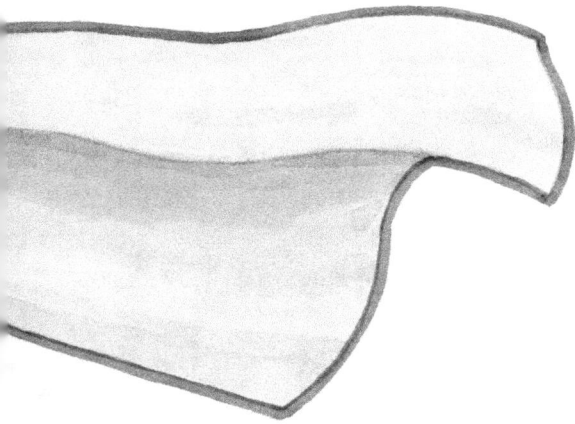

He was always the first to reach the playground. He
never finished his breakfast because he was in a hurry
to reach the playground.
He would take his bicycle and ride as fast as he could.
All he wanted to do was play all day.

He sat on the swing and flew high. 'Whee!' shouted Lobo, it's so much fun. 'Don't go up so high,' Lucy said. But Lobo did not listen. He did not stop swinging until he began to feel sick.

He loved to climb trees. But he forgot to be careful and scraped his knees. Oh, how badly his knees hurt.

His feet became too sore from running around with his friends.
Even when Lobo was really tired, he would not stop playing.

One day, there was a party at Lobo's house. He cycled through the neighbourhood inviting his friends.

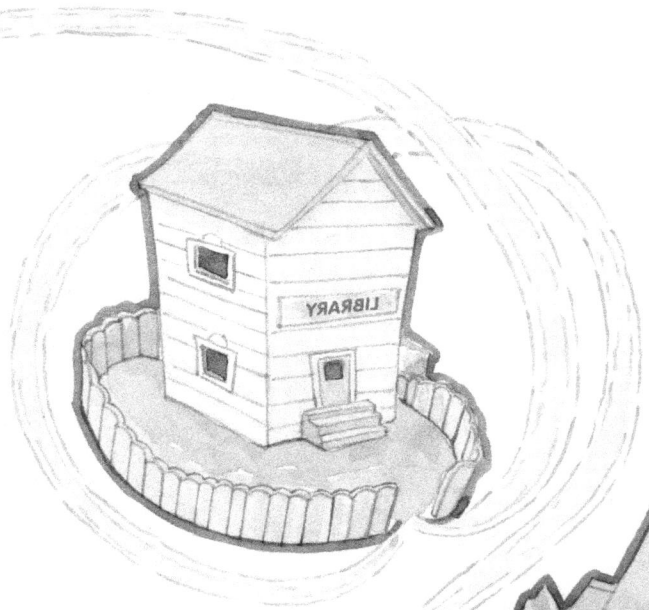

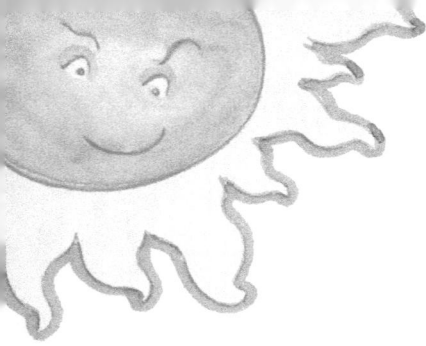

How tired he was, cycling around all day in the sun! And he had burnt his skin too. Lobo's skin became all red.

'Oh dear! I hope I don't get blisters!' thought Lobo. Lobo wondered if he should tell his mother how tired he felt. But he decided to wait until the party was over.

At the party, Lobo played with his friends for hours even though his body was already sore. He finally stopped when his legs could not run anymore.

Lobo sang and danced too.
He sang so many songs
that his throat became
hoarse. 'Oh dear, what have
I done?' His forehead felt
hot too.

At the end of the party,
Lobo was very tired.
He wished he had not
run about so much and
sung so loudly.

His whole body hurt from all that he had done that day. He began to cry. Mother came and tucked him into bed. 'Your body needs rest,' she said kindly.

'I should start taking care of myself and my body,' thought Lobo.

The next morning Lobo woke up feeling better. He promised his parents that he would behave better. He finished all his meals and never played for too long. Lobo became healthier. He was less tired and he enjoyed his games more too!

Wash! Wash! Wash!

It was a hot summer day. Jane had spent the whole afternoon at the playground. She was feeling so sweaty and dirty!

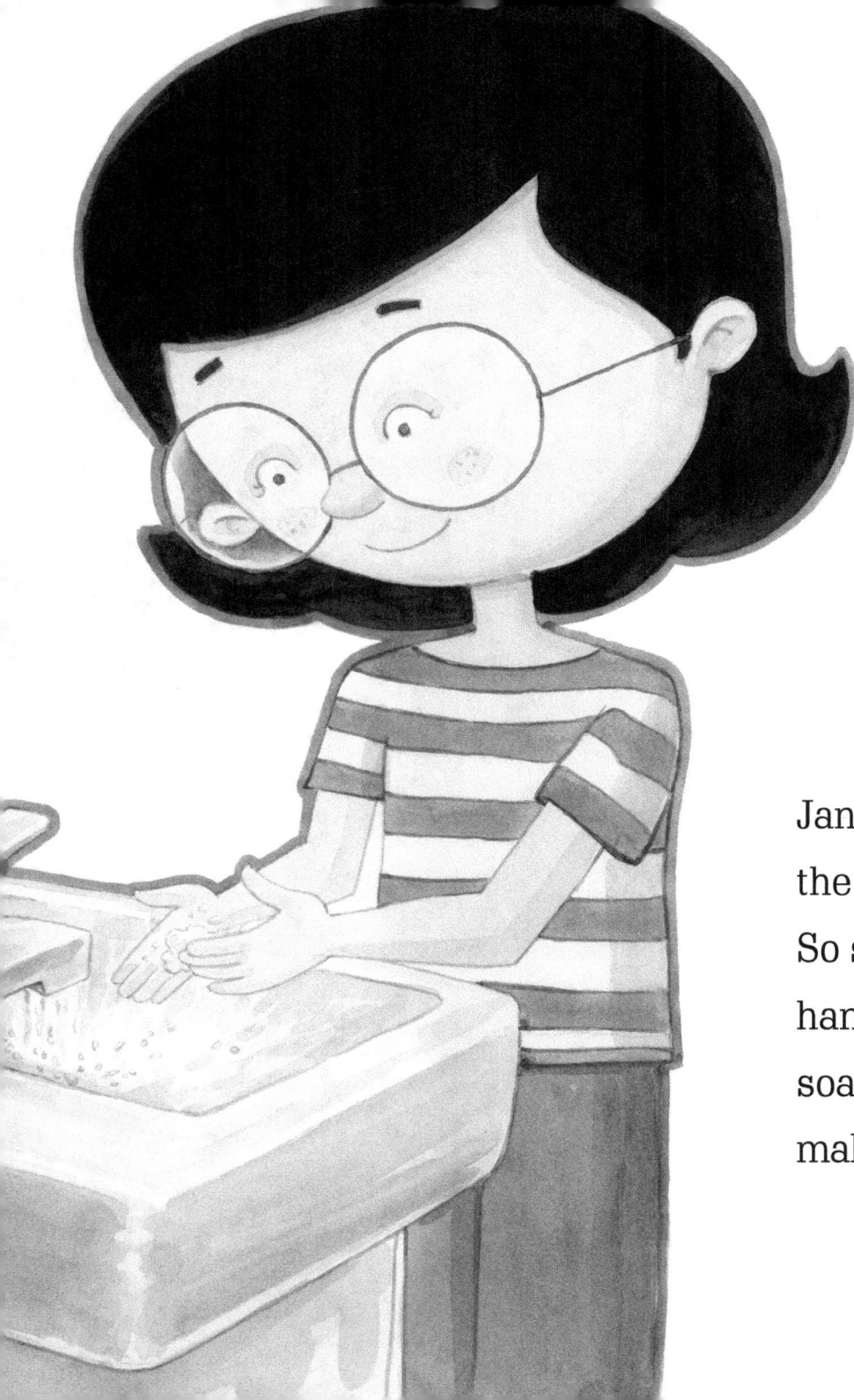

Jane could almost feel the germs on her body! So she washed her hands thoroughly with soap. But that did not make her feel better.

'Oh bother!' she said, 'My hands are clean but my face is sweaty!' So she took out her fruity face wash and spread it on her face.

Then she rinsed her
face thoroughly. Her
face felt so clean! 'Oh
bother!' said Jane
again, 'But my legs and
feet are still dirty!'

And so Jane sat down on a bathroom stool and washed her feet with water. Then she took out a large dollop of soap and spread it on her legs.

Her legs and feet were clean now! But her body back and tummy and neck were still sweaty. 'Well then I guess its best I take a shower!' thought Jane.

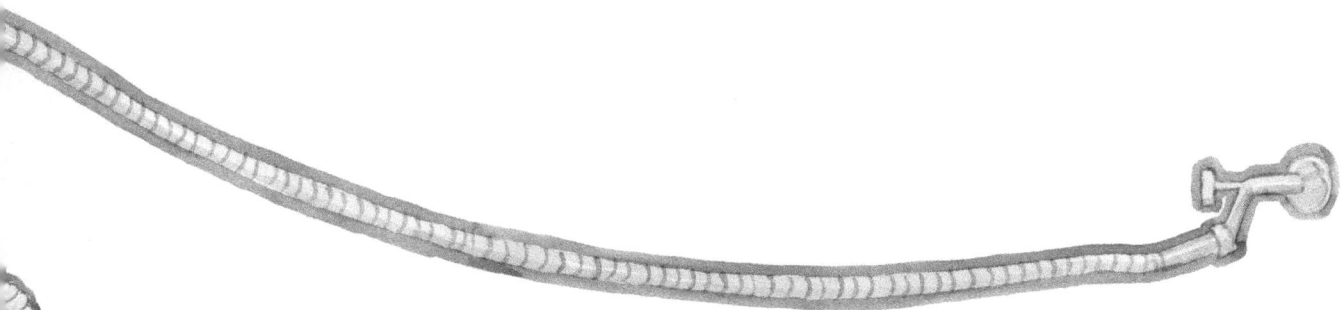

First Jane filled her bathtub with warm water. Then she poured her bubble bath soap into it. Soon her bathtub was full of bubbles!

Jane sat happily in the
bubble bath and rubbed
her whole body with soap.
She put soap on her tummy,
arms and legs. But she just
could not reach her back!

'I can reach my back with my loofah!' thought Jane, 'And scrubbing my skin with the loofah will really remove the dirt and germs!' thought Jane.

So Jane took out her loofah. Then she gently scrubbed her back, neck, shoulders and soles with it! How clean she felt!

But Jane had another problem.
'My hair is still sweaty and full of
germs!' she thought. So she took out
her favourite bottle of shampoo.

She poured a dollop of it on her wet hair and worked it up to froth. When she felt her hair was clean enough, Jane washed out all the shampoo from her hair.

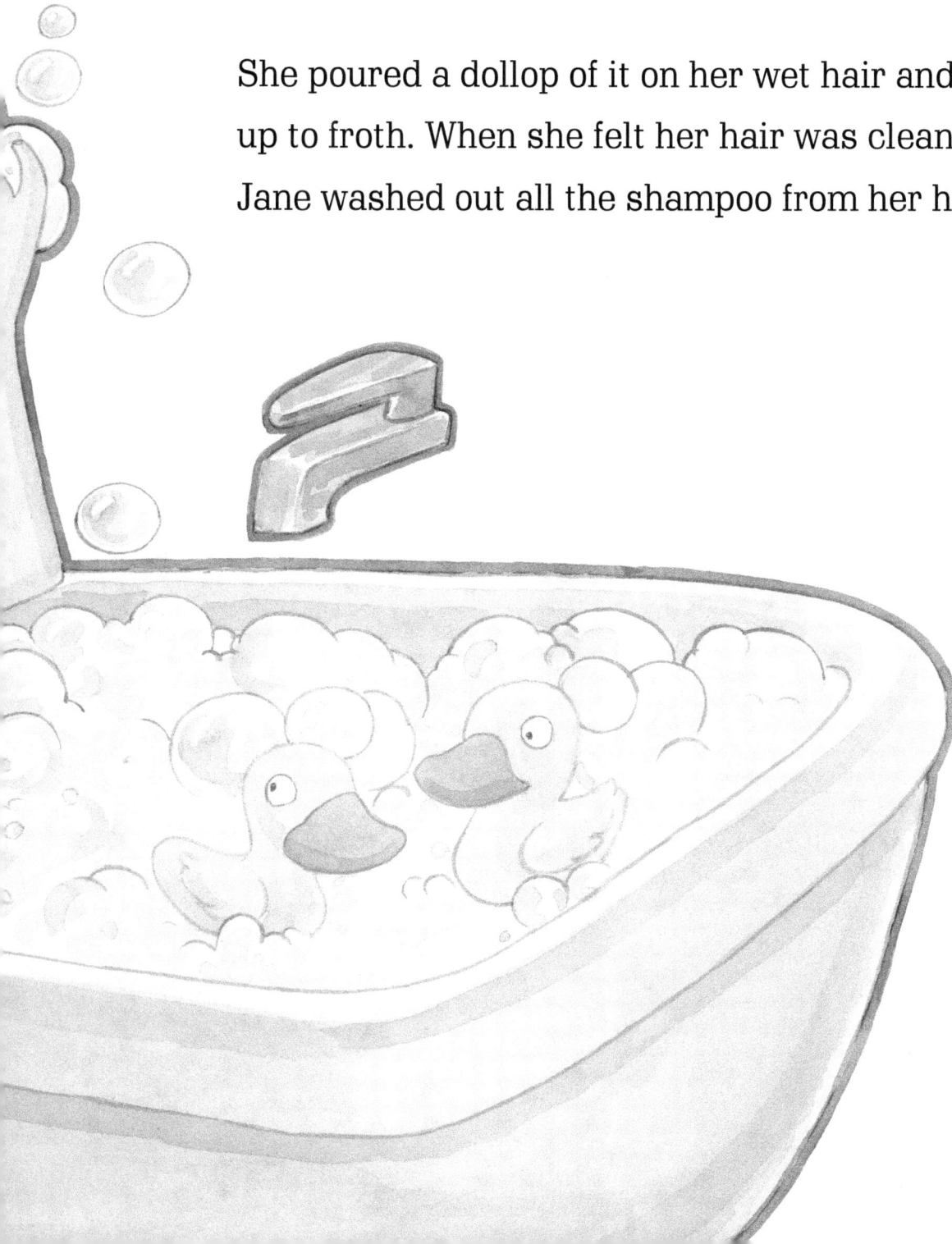

When Jane was out of the bathtub, she said, 'The bath has given me new energy!' How wonderful it was to feel so fresh and clean!

Jane had really enjoyed her
bubble bath! She hummed
happily as she dried her hair.

'I have washed away all the germs from my body!' said Jane. Then she walked confidently out of the bathroom, feeling cleaner than ever.

www.ingramcontent.com/pod-product-compliance
Lightning Source LLC
LaVergne TN
LVHW082324080426
835508LV00042B/1533